Howard Katz

Patrick Marber was born in 1964. He lives in London.

PATRICK MARBER

Howard Katz

ff

faber and faber

First published in 2001
by Faber and Faber Limited
3 Queen Square, London WC1N 3AU

Typeset by Country Setting, Kingsdown, Kent CT14 8ES
Printed in England by Mackays of Chatham plc, Chatham, Kent

'Leaning on a Lamp-Post'
Words and music by Noel Gay © 1937 Richard Armitage Ltd,
8–9 Frith Street, London W1. Used by permission of Music Sales Ltd.
All rights reserved. International copyright secure.

A CIP record for this book
is available from the British Library

0-571-21005-8

2 4 6 8 10 9 7 5 3 1

For my son

Acknowledgements

My grateful thanks to all those
who helped me with this play, especially
Robert Fox, Debra Gillett, Scott Rudin,
Max Stafford-Clark and all at
the National Theatre, London

Above all, to Ron Cook
and the original company of actors
who performed *Howard Katz*:
my thanks and my love

P.M.
July 2001

Howard Katz was first performed in the Cottesloe
auditorium of the National Theatre, London, on
1 June 2001, with the following cast:

Howard Katz Ron Cook
Natalie, Marcia, Cheryl, Dealer Ashley Jensen
Ellie, May, Linda Cherry Morris
Jo, Mr Lord, Orderly, Lou Trevor Peacock
Bernie, Jim, Greg, Martin, Fred, Pit Boss Paul Ritter
Norman, Waiter, Security Guard, Inspector
   Nadim Sawalha
Jess, Viv, Tina, Mother, Manager Mossie Smith
Robin, Ricky, Bell Boy, Felix, Waiter Russell Tovey
Ollie, Boy Elian Lloyd Smith/Benedict Smith

Director Patrick Marber
Designer Rob Howell
Lighting Hugh Vanstone
Music Adrian Johnston
Sound Christopher Shutt
Assistant Director Steven James Little

Characters

Howard Katz, fifty or thereabouts
Robin, early twenties
Jo, Katz's father, around seventy
Bernie, Katz's brother, forties
Ellie, Katz's mother, around seventy
Ollie, Katz's son, nine or ten
Jess, Katz's wife, forties
Norman, a barber, sixties
Natalie, Bernie's girlfriend,
Katz's client, around thirty
Marcia, Katz's assistant
Ricky Barnes, Katz's client, twenties
Casino Waiter 1
Viv, a TV producer
Jim, a TV producer
May
Greg, Katz's boss
Tina, an agent in the same company
Bell Boy
Mr Lord
Cheryl
Martin
Felix
Boy
Mother
Security Guard
Hospital Orderly

Fred
Inspector
Dealer
Pit Boss
Casino Waiter 2
Lou
Linda
Manager

The play is set in London.

Time

The present and the past.
The action of the play occurs
over one and a half years.

The action should occur continuously,
without blackouts between scenes.

It should seem as if the protagonist
is in a dream – though he isn't.

The play can be acted by a cast of nine:
five men, three women, one boy.

It can be performed with a larger cast
but not a smaller one.

The doubling of roles is sometimes significant.
Where this is so it is detailed in the text.

HOWARD KATZ

Act One

Present.

A Park. Dawn.

Figures in silhouette.

Dissolve.

Reveal Katz asleep on a bench.

He wakes from a bad dream, fighting the air.

He looks about. Remembers where he is.

He checks his watch. Looks at his grey plastic bag.

He finds a white yarmulke in his pocket and wipes his face with it.

He looks up to the sky, grimaces at God, puts the yarmulke on.

He lights a cigarette.

A young man (Robin) wanders past and approaches him.

Robin Hey, mate. Mate? You got a spare?

> *Katz, with vague disdain, removes the cigarette from his mouth and holds it up for Robin to take.*

Not if it's your last one . . .

> *Katz brandishes the cigarette.*

I'm not having it if you're reluctant.

Katz Yes or no?

Robin Nahh, you're *reluctant*.

Katz I *was* reluctant, I'm not any more. Take it.

Robin Nahh, I've imposed.

> *Katz shrugs and takes a drag. The young man watches him.*

Katz *What?*

Robin You wanna go somewhere?

Katz Eh?

Robin *Go* somewhere.

Katz Oh. No.

Robin Twenny quid, suck your cock.

Katz It's six o'clock in the morning. Will you piss off for a fiver?

Robin Yeah, I can do that.

> *Katz hands him £5.*

Give us your wallet.

Katz No.

Robin Go on, you can afford it.

Katz Is this a mugging or a guilt trip?

> *Beat.*

Robin Give us a fag.

Katz Will you leave me alone, *please.*

Robin Give us a fag then.

Katz hands him a cigarette from his packet.

Robin mimes he needs a light.

Katz throws him a book of matches. Robin reads.

'Casino.' Big winner, were you?

Katz does not respond.

What you doing here?

Katz I'm thinking.

Robin Oh yeah? 'Bout what?

Pause.

Katz Suicide.

Pause.

Robin 'Cos you lost?

Katz (*slight smile*) No.

Robin Don't do it, mate.

Katz Oh, really?

Robin Nahh, you might regret it.

Katz sighs.

Suit yourself, I'm just being nice.

Katz Know a bit about the subject, do you?

Robin (*levelly*) Yeah.

Beat.

Katz Here . . .

Katz hands him his wallet. Robin rifles through it. He finds some photos.

Robin This your family?

Katz nods. Robin offers the wallet back.

Katz Keep it.

Katz hands Robin his wristwatch.

Robin You sure . . .?

Katz nods. Robin looks at Katz, a little concerned.

Nice hat.

Katz removes his yarmulke, offers it to Robin.

Nahh, you're alright.

Katz puts the yarmulke in his pocket. Robin stands.

Ta then.

Katz D'you want some breakfast . . .?

Robin . . . Where?

Katz . . . McDonald's . . .?

Robin You're not police?

Katz No.

Robin looks at Katz, thinks.

Robin I said I'd meet someone . . . sorry. Take it easy, right?

Robin exits.

Katz thinks. Looks in his grey plastic bag.

In the distance, a car alarm is going off . . .

As the alarm increases in volume, Katz remembers . . .

The next scene assembles around him.

A barber's shop. A Saturday, around 1 p.m.
The past.

Katz finds car keys in his pocket and presses a
button. The alarm stops.

Katz What do you give the man who has everything?

Bern Nothing.

Katz You give him what he *deserves*. You – give –
him – *nothing*.

Bern (*gestures outside*) They've set it too sensitive.

Katz (*pockets the keys*) A butterfly farts in the
Philippines and my alarm goes off. Sorry, Norm.

Norm Get back in this chair, young man.

Bernie (Bern, Katz's brother) continues sweeping
up. Norman (Norm) continues finishing off Katz's
hair at the back. Josef Katz (Jo, Katz's father) is
putting gel on Ollie's hair (Ollie is Katz's son,
aged ten).

All three barbers wear jackets with 'Jo', 'Norm' and
'Bern' stitched on their respective breast pockets.
Ellie (Katz's mother) sits at the till.

Jo D'you know this boy's got three crowns?

Katz Yep, takes after me.

Jo D'you know what it *means*? To have 'three crowns'?

Ollie No?

Jo It means you've got three crowns.

Norm Sorry, did I give you a nick?

Katz No, no.

Bern picks up a ukulele from the counter. Starts to play.

Bern So I said, 'It's a "piece", not a "tool".'

Katz What is?

Bern A gun. It's a *piece*, not a tool.

Katz So what's a tool?

Bern A blunt object.

Katz I thought a knife was a 'tool'?

Bern No. A *knife* is a *blade*.

Ellie Bernard, that's not very nice.

Norm (*brushing Katz down*) OK?

Katz Yeah, lovely. Thanks, Norm.

Norm My pleasure.

Norm starts sweeping up. Shop bell rings. Natalie (Nat) enters.

Nat Hi, Ellie.

Ellie Hello, love.

Bern Hello, darling.

Natalie kisses him.

Nat Have you finished? Oh, I love watching you work.

Bern Aphrodisiac is it? A man and his clippers.

Nat Oh yes. Hey, Howard, is that the new car?

Katz Yes indeed, what d'you think?

Nat I think you're a *swinger*.

Katz Tragic, isn't it?

Bern If I didn't like him, I'd despise him.

Katz I know *exactly* what you mean.

Ellie You two going to the match?

Nat Yes . . .

Ellie D'you like football?

Nat No, not really. You?

Ellie I used to go. But I stopped.

Nat Why?

Ellie It was the noise. And the smell.

Ollie Who are they playing?

Bern Notts Forest.

Jo I remember when football was a *game*.

Bern Off he goes . . .

Jo Not a knees-up for corporate sponsors.

Bern Howie, you should get some footballers.

Katz No time for big egos, mate – too busy with this one. (*He gestures to Natalie.*)

Nat So how come I'm not working, Mr Agent?

Katz I'm dealing with it!

Jo (*to Nat*) But I saw you on telly, last night.

Nat It's a repeat.

Jo What are they repeating it for?

Bern Dad!

Jo I liked *you* but I can't say I liked the programme. Who was that bloke with the spike in his face?

Nat He's a singer, he's popular with the 'young people'.

Jo Is he? When we were young, we were *protesting*.

Katz What's it like, having principles?

Jo (*mock sorrow*) It's a constant burden.

Bern What were *you* doin', up at midnight?

Jo I couldn't sleep, your mother was snoring.

Ellie I don't snore.

Jo Fifty years, she's never snored. (*to Ollie*) What d'you reckon, Sir?

Ollie Yeah. Thanks, Grandpa.

Katz (*to Ollie*) You're a sensation.

Ellie Very smart, Ollie.

Jo On the house.

Katz Dad . . .

Jo 'Course.

Katz approaches Ellie to slip her some money.
Jo notices:

Howard. Put your wallet away. I said, 'On the house.'

Suddenly, everyone 'freezes' except Katz. He stares
at his wallet (the one he gave 'Robin'). He gazes at
his family.

The action resumes as the shop bell rings.

Katz Here she is!

Jess (Katz's wife) enters with shopping bags. Katz
kisses her.

My love, let me help you.

Jess Thanks. (*She ruffles his hair.*) Hallo, peanut.

Ellie Thanks, Jess.

Jess Pleasure. (*to Ollie*) Look at you! Who's the
artist?

Ollie Grandpa.

Jo We try.

Jess Hey Nat, great hair.

Nat Oh, thanks.

Jess Really great.

Nat Thanks. Bern hates it.

Jess Why?

Nat 'Cos he didn't cut it.

Jess Don't ever let him.

Nat I won't.

Bern (*to Katz*) Aren't women the business?

Katz No, just these two.

Bern (*to Nat*) Are we skedaddlin' or what?

Nat I'm waiting for *you*. Come on.

  Bern notices Ollie watching them.

Bern (*to Ollie*) Ol, you wanna come to a game
sometime?

Ollie (*to Jess*) Can I?

Jess 'Course you can.

Bern (*to Ollie*) It's a date. 'Bye all!

Nat (*to Katz*) Howard . . .

Katz (*to Nat, gesturing phone*) Next week, yeah?

Nat Yeah, see ya.

  Bern and Natalie exit.

Katz How *does* he do it?

Jess He's attractive.

Katz Just 'cos he likes sex doesn't make him sexy.

Jess It *helps*.

Jo (*kisses Ellie*) He learnt from the *king*, that's the
secret.

Ellie (*to Jess*) They don't mature, they just get older.

Jess Jo, good as new, did it myself.

She hands Jo a wristwatch – the one Katz gave 'Robin' in the previous scene.

Jo Jessie, thank you. What was wrong with it?

Jess Your balance spring – don't ask, it's fixed.

Jo (*shows Ollie*) One day, this'll be yours. It's very old, it was my dad's.

Ollie It's too big for me . . .

Jo It won't be when you get it.

Ollie When's that?

Jo looks at Katz. Katz looks at Jess.

Jess When you're old.

Jo I'll look after it, then your dad and then you.

Jo puts the watch on, strums the ukulele: 'Leaning on a Lamp-Post'.

Jess (*to Ellie*) Shall I help you upstairs?

Ellie Would you? Thanks. (*to Ollie*) D'you want to carry this, darling?

Ellie carries a bag off. Ollie follows with a bag.

Jess picks up hers. Katz approaches her. Puts his arms round her.

Katz Hello . . .

Jess Are you alright? (*to Jo*) Is he alright?

Jo 'Course not, he's *fifty*.

She laughs, exits. Katz watches his father playing for a while.

Jo looks up, smiles at Katz.

Norman is now ready to leave. Katz slips him a £10 tip.

Norm See you Monday, Jo.

Jo Have a good weekend, Sir. Up to anything?

Norm Golf with my brother.

Jo *Mazel tov*, hope you murder 'im.

Norm 'Bye, Howard.

Katz (*points to his hair*) Thanks.

Norm Any time.

Jo Hey Norm, *sorry*, do us a favour and count the cash? (*to Katz*) You coming up?

Katz nods. Jo exits.

Katz sits in a barber's chair. He looks at Norm counting the cash.

Katz starts to cry. Norman looks up. Katz hides his face.

Norm Howard? What's the matter?

Katz (*softly*) I've no idea. I've absolutely no idea.

Marcia enters. We are now in Katz's office. A desk, computer, papers, etc.

Marcia Good morning, Mr Katz.

Katz Who are you?

Marcia I'm Marcia, I'm your new assistant.

Katz Great. Get me forty Dunhill.

Marcia exits. Phone rings. Katz picks up.

(*in phone*) Phil! Phil – you'll *love* this: JASON BOYCE.
(*Katz laughs.*) You're lovin' it already!? WAIT! Jason
fucking Boyce says to me, 'You know, *Howard*, you
can have too much sex, drugs and rock 'n' roll.
I'm *bored* of the parties, the press, the paparazzi,
the dribbling, gibbering autograph-hunters.'
On and on he's going, *verbing* away like a friggin' *drill*.
Yeah, the full *thesaurus* of celebrity bullshit '*agony*'.
So *finally*, finally fucking *finally*, he says, 'Howard . . .
I'm gonna *change my life*: I'm gonna go live in *Tibet*
for a *year*. Just sit in a wigwam and *chill*. Maybe learn
to play the *flute*.' (*Katz gurgles with delight.*) I say,
'*Great!* Do it *Jase*, whatever makes you *happy*.'
He says, 'You know, I'm gonna *go* for it. I'm really
gonna *go* for it.'
So what did he *do*? You wanna know?
He's just signed up for twelve weeks in Swansea.
Fuckin' PANTO!!
'PUSS IN BOOTS'!!!
No. I don't know if it's *fully cast*.

*He puts the phone down. Marcia enters. She has
been running.*

Marcia Your cigarettes, Mr Katz.

Katz goes down on one knee.

Katz Please excuse my *unpleasantness*, earlier.

Marcia Oh, no, no, no, Mr Katz.

Katz (*seeing the cigarettes*) Do I have *breasts*? (*He waves the packets.*) These are *lights*, I smoke the real ones.

Marcia It won't happen again.

Katz Do I have a lunch?

Marcia Barry Cox, he just called to confirm.

Katz Why d'you think Barry Cox wants lunch?

Marcia I–I–I'm so sorry, who is Barry Cox?

Katz Exactly! So why does he want lunch?

Marcia M–maybe for you to . . . *help* him?

Katz *Yes.* To *help* him. He is seeking my representation because he's '*all washed up*'. What will I say when he asks for my 'help'?

Marcia M–maybe that you'll . . . *think* about it?

Katz Correct. I will say I will *think* about it. *Meaning*?

Marcia Meaning you won't?

Katz *Good.* Sit. In this business, if someone says to you that they will 'think about it', their answer will be 'No'. That which requires our *thought* is undesirable. 'The world is a turd and we are but flies.' You wanna do this hideous job?

Marcia I think so, I mean if –

Katz You wanna come for lunch with me and Baz?

Marcia Well . . . I – I'd like to . . . but I have a lot of –

Katz FINISH THESE SENTENCES. Really.

The internal phone rings. Katz gestures Marcia to answer it.

Marcia (*in phone*) Mr Katz's office, Marcia speaking . . . Thank you. (*to Katz*) Ricky Barnes is in reception.

Katz (*surprised*) Is he now? One day – maybe even *this* day – Little Ricky Barnes will attempt to ferret his way into your lacy knickers. *Beware*. The Boy Is Riddled.

Marcia I'm *engaged*.

Katz *Usher*.

Marcia exits. Katz's mobile rings. He looks at the display, grimaces, takes the call.

(*in phone*) Melanie! (*He listens for a while.*) The truth?
Are you *sure*?
Really truly sure?
OK. Here's the reason you don't *work*: you've had too much *work*.
On your face. Yes.
Of course people *know*.
Of course they *know*.
How? YOU CAN'T FROWN.
The frown is a very expressive gesture, babe.
No it isn't? Yes It Is.
And since we're here: your teeth are too big for your mouth and your lips are too big for your face. EAT SOME FOOD – you're like a skull on a *stick*.
The Camera *Hates* You. That's Why You Don't *Work*.
I'm not being cruel. You *asked* me.

Well, feel sad then.
I didn't do *anything*. You did it to yourself.

Marcia shows in Ricky Barnes (Ricky). He is wearing shades.

Marcia Mr Katz, Ricky's here.

Katz Hi! *Hey*, you've lost *weight*. You look *delicious*.

Ricky Do I? Thanks.

Katz *Du thé* or *du café*?

Ricky No, thanks.

Katz (*to Marcia*) Exit.

Marcia exits. Katz strokes Ricky's suit.

What *is* this? Armani? Versace? Or did an angel weave it in heaven?

Ricky It's Hugo Boss.

Katz And most *splendid* it is – I could eat you.

Ricky Sorry to bust in, unannounced. You OK, timewise?

Katz Always time for *cliente numero uno*. By the way, young Sir, we banked a *vigorous* cheque for you: the *ad* – you funky, rapping chicken you!

Katz squawks 'rap' style. Then trails off as he realises something's wrong . . .

Ricky I'm unhappy.

Pause.

Katz How unhappy?

Ricky I'm *very* unhappy.

Phone rings, Katz picks up.

Katz (*in phone*) Fuck off. (*to Ricky*) Why?

Ricky You're . . . you can be rude. Sometimes.

Katz Excuse me?

Ricky People . . . in the business, think you're rude. At meetings people say, 'How's Howard?' They roll their eyes.

Katz You're throwing six years down the toilet 'cos people roll their *eyes*?

Ricky I just want – for this next *phase* in my career – to be with someone who isn't so *aggressive*.

Katz IT'S MY JOB, IT'S WHAT I DO. I'm the bastard so *you* look *sweet*, it's called 'representation'.

Ricky Yeah, but, you know, all this losing your temper at people . . . it's . . . it's a bit *nineties*. The business is changing, H.

Katz 'The *business*?' You're a *child*. THERE'S NO SUN TODAY.

Ricky removes his shades.

Thank you. Rick, what is it? You think I don't understand, I'm too old?

Ricky No –

Katz I *am* old – I'm as old as the wheel – and The Wheel *Works*.

Ricky Howard –

Katz Ricky, Ricky, Ricky. Ricky. *Darren*. Six years ago, what *were* you?

Ricky Howard –

Katz You were a *plumber's mate*, Darren. You were 'a cheeky plumber's mate' in a DIY show on Channel *Nowhere*. Now, you're *almost* a National Phenomenon. You know what *happened* to you? *Me*.

Ricky And I'm totally *grateful* for everything you done but everybody needs a change –

Katz *I* don't.

Ricky I'm gutted, but this is how it is.

   Pause.

Katz You're breaking my heart, you know that? (*resigned*) Who?

Ricky Georgina Freeman.

Katz She was my *PA*. She's a *Sloane* with a *phone*.

Ricky She's actually really respected.

Katz When she's *there*, when she's not at *lunch* or *between marriages* – she's got *four kids*, she's a *busy woman*. Uncle Howard is here for you day and night.

Ricky I've made my decision, I'm sorry.

Katz No you're not, you're *relieved*. But you 'did it in person' and for that I thank you.

Ricky It's the *least* I could do, Howard. I want you to know that I know I wouldn't be where I am without you.

Katz I say this in anger, not bitterness – there's a distinction, it's a useful one: You Have No Talent. You've been very lucky you've had a brilliant agent –

Ricky tries to speak.

– you'll disagree because you have to. But the truth is you're not intelligent enough to understand how and why this business works. You are a bubble and you will burst. Please know that I'm not *sad* to lose you, I was merely 'affecting sadness', as a *courtesy*.

Ricky sits, stunned.

Hey, scram, *Goldenballs*. You've got a whole new life to screw up, get to it. I'm *busy*. Helping people.

Night. Jo and Ellie's flat. Katz and his father are playing backgammon at the kitchen table.

Jo Lover's Leap.

Katz You wanna double?

Jo I accept your double. And I'm a fool.

Katz turns the doubling dice over. They play a little more.

Jo stops. He looks at Katz.

You're mother's back soon. I have no one I can tell this to, so I'm telling *you* . . . and I'm *sorry* to tell you . . . but I have to tell *someone* . . .

I go to *shul*, on Yom Kippur, I atone. It doesn't help. I . . . there's a woman . . . who I love. Who I have loved a long time.

Katz How long?

Jo *Years*. Many years. On and off.

Katz Hmm . . .

Jo Alright . . . ?

Katz Yes . . .

Jo And . . . four weeks ago, she tells me it's finished. She's found a man who can marry her. And . . . now . . . I don't want to live. I feel my life is ended.

Katz Why didn't you leave Mum?

Jo I made a vow . . . before *God*, to be with her.

Katz You were *kids*, Dad, when you married, *virgins*. Different world.

Jo Same God.

Pause.

Katz What's her name?

Jo May.

Katz Jewish?

Jo shakes his head.

Younger woman?

Jo No. A little. She's sixty-four.

Katz Does Mum know?

Jo She knows. We're not . . . passionate.

Katz Tell me about it.

Jo You and Jess?

22

Katz Sometimes . . . I think my dick is the smallest thing in the world.

Jo Your brother: biggest *shlonger* in London.

Katz Smallest brain, though.

Jo Will you do a *mitzvah* for me?

Katz 'Course I will.

Jo I warn you, it's a *big* mitzvah: I've decided I'm gonna be cremated –

Katz Dad –

Jo I know, it's not allowed, I know. But . . . my soul . . . doesn't deserve to go to God –

Katz You've paid burial rights for *years*.

Jo For which I get to go to *Willesden*. Big deal. Maybe they'll let me transfer it – you wanna go to Willesden?

Katz Dad . . .

Jo So I'm going Reform, OK?

Katz Hey, listen, *I* don't mind. I haven't been to *shul* since –

Jo Your bar mitzvah, this we know. So . . . I know you're busy and everything but . . . will you learn to say Kaddish? So when you're doing the . . . with the ashes, you can say Kaddish for me?

Katz I can't read Hebrew, Dad. I've forgotten it.

Jo So I'll teach you, we can do it with the – where they give you the sounds.

Katz Phonetics.

Jo You'll do this?

Katz Sure. In *twenty* years when you're at *dying* age.

Jo We'll do it soon, please. Take an hour or two. (*Jo looks at Katz, troubled.*) So *now* what d'you think of your father?

> *Pause.*

Katz I don't *disapprove*, if you're . . . worried about that.

Jo No?

Katz *No.* But Dad, don't say you don't want to *live. Everyone* feels . . . sometimes. The pain will pass.

> *Katz puts his arms round his father. Jo starts to cry. Katz holds him.*

> *Night. A casino. Katz is with his mother. She has a small pile of chips (about £70).*

Ellie What can I do, I'm lucky. Always have been.

Katz Yeah?

Ellie Always.

Katz What's the secret then?

Ellie To luck? Knowing when it's gone.

> *A Waiter approaches.*

Waiter Sir? Madam?

Ellie Coffee, please.

Katz Me too, thank you.

Waiter Two coffees.

Waiter exits.

Ellie Jessie tells me you've been in a . . . what is it?

Katz Flotation tank. She *made* me go. It's like . . . it's a dark . . . *pod*, full of salt water. And you lie there, naked, on your back, and they play classical music or birds twittering and you relax.

Ellie They change the water, between the 'floaters'?

Katz I dunno, I s'pose so.

Ellie You should *ask*. How can you relax in someone else's water?

Katz Well I *didn't*.

Ellie I'm not surprised.

Katz I couldn't relax because –

Ellie You're stressed, always have been.

Katz Have I?

Ellie Always. You're a *worrier*. Bernard, his head could be falling off, he's smiling.

Katz So, I lay in this tank, today, and . . . I had too many *thoughts*. I couldn't be calm – I couldn't be *still*. I started *screaming*, they had to let me out.

Ellie You're not unhappy with Jess?

Katz No, 'course not. (*Shakes his head.*) Sometimes . . . I think I've never done a *thing* . . .

Ellie You've got a wonderful *son*, Howard.

Katz He needs his mum.

Ellie Every son needs his father.

Katz What did I *want*, when I was a kid?

Ellie You wanted to drive a bus. Then you wanted to be a spy. Then a policeman. And then a tramp. *So?*

Katz So don't worry, I'm fine.

Ellie You don't look it. Do something, *change* things.

Katz I don't have the time to think *how*. Where – where can a Jew go to contemplate his life? A goy can check into a monastery, where can a Jew go?

Ellie To the jungle.

Katz Eh?

Ellie Go on safari. Take yourself on a trip like . . . Lou, *Lou Grossman*. You know Linda – *kalooki Linda* – her Lou went to Africa. They do these . . . 'packages'. He came back like a young man. He does archery now.

Katz Mum, I don't want to go to the jungle with Lou Grossman.

Ellie He's *been*. He's not going again. Just promise you won't go on kibbutz.

Katz I promise.

Ellie (*wistfully*) They never come back . . .

    Beat.

Katz *Who?*

Ellie Doctors, dentists, lawyers. They go and pick oranges the rest of their lives.

Katz (*snaps*) Where d'you *get* this shit? Sorry. Sorry.

Ellie I just want you to be content. Not even happy. Content is enough.

> *Katz looks at her, she looks away, he squeezes her hand.*

Katz You wanna play some more?

Ellie No, I'll cash in. How much d'you lose?

Katz Two grand.

Ellie Can you afford it?

Katz Nope.

Ellie You should play smaller.

Katz Nyahh, I'd get bored.

> *Ellie pushes her chips to him.*

Mum . . .

Ellie Take it.

Katz It's *yours*, you won it.

Ellie I'll win again, I *want* you to have it.

Katz Don't be silly.

Ellie (*sadly*) Will you please . . . *take something* from me? Just once in your life?

> *Pause.*

Katz OK. (*gently*) Thank you. Mum? *Thank you.*

Ellie Go and cash in. I'll be outside.

Ellie exits. Katz slowly collects her chips. The Waiter returns.

Waiter Two coffees.

Katz Too late. But thank you.

Katz puts all the chips on the Waiter's tray.

Waiter Sir??

Katz Enjoy.

Waiter Thank you, Sir.

A drinking club. Katz arrives. His client, Natalie, is sitting with Jim and Viv (two TV producers).

Jim Cometh the hour, cometh the Howard!

Katz Jim! Viv! Hi, Nat.

Jim Your wonderful client has been *regaling* us.

Viv Funny is funny and *she is funny.*

Jim *Very* funny.

Viv And *angry.*

Jim We *love* the anger.

Nat (*slightly worried*) Do I seem *angry*?

Jim *Witty* angry: acerbic. Your video reviews, on that . . . *programme* – hilarious!

Viv So much television these days, so much *everything* is–is–is . . . *bland.*

Jim We Hate Bland.

Viv So this meeting –

Jim This *conversation* –

Viv This *drink* . . . is – *Viv*, 'cut to the *chase*': Jim and I have a commission, for a new show, late night. It's called 'The Pulse' –

Jim Or maybe just 'Pulse' . . .

Viv Actually . . . (*to Natalie*) which do *you* prefer?

Nat Err . . . '*The* Pulse'.

Viv (*to Jim*) See, it's better!

Jim A female conspiracy! Howard, stick up for the blokes!

Katz '*The*'.

Jim I Stand Defeated! Actually, 'The Powers That Be' wanted us to call it 'Club Zeitgeist' – we're like, excuse me, No Way. Though, actually, *tonally – ironically* – it will *be* quite 'zeitgeisty' but you don't wanna go around screaming about it, do you?

   Beat.

Nat What is it?

Viv We're still developing the format but basically 'The Pulse' is a magazine show set in a different club each week: different rooms, different *things* happening . . .

Jim Music, comedy, politics, celebrities, *criminals*: 'sexyfunnyscary'. It sounds crap but it's kind of our mantra . . .

Viv *So* . . .

Jim Ricky Barnes is already on board but we need a hip young gunslinger riding shotgun. (*to Nat*) D'you know Ricky?

Nat Yeah . . . I met him at . . . he's lovely.

Jim He's the *future*.

Viv So . . . 'The Big *So*' . . .

Jim (*to Nat*) We think *you're* the future *too*, I mean, I personally, would *love* to work with you . . .

Viv Bottom line: how d'ya fancy co-presenting 'The Pulse'?

Natalie glances at Katz.

Katz I think it's a 'no'. It's a 'no'. Thank you.

Pause.

Jim *Right*. OK . . .

Viv Any reason . . .?

Jim We *learn* from you . . .

Katz I think it's because . . . you are cynical peddlers of *shite*.

Silence.

(*Panicking*) I'm joking! I was *joking*! Of course we're interested. Nat?

Nat Yeah, absolutely.

Jim Christ, you *bastard*!

Katz (*to Viv*) Talk later, yeah? (*He raises his glass.*)

All 'The Pulse'!

Katz is at the zoo with his son, Ollie. They are at the penguin pool.

Ollie Dad . . .

Katz Hey, Ol, d'you fancy an ice cream?

Ollie No thanks.

Pause.

Katz What d'you think of these penguins?

Ollie They might be sad . . .

Katz Why?

Ollie Because they're birds but they can't fly.

Katz Hey . . . they . . . they don't *know* that. They're not *sad*, they've got it good, they're just waiting for a herring or something, they're OK.

Ollie nods, unconvinced.

Have you got homework to do, this weekend?

Ollie Geography project.

Katz What d'you have to do?

Ollie Make a map of where we live.

Katz The streets and houses and stuff?

Ollie nods.

You gonna use colours?

Ollie nods.

Good for you.

They sit down.

So . . . Mum told me about what's happening at school . . . and . . . guess what, when I was your age, a little older, same thing happened to me.

Ollie Why?

Katz 'Cos I was a titch. And no good at sports. And because I'm a Jew. They used to say, 'Katz is barking,' you know, 'mad'? And they'd steal my bag, hit me, gimme a dead leg, you know?

Ollie Yeah.

Katz So . . . your grandpa taught me and your Uncle Bernie how to *fight*. We used to practise at home when your grandma thought we were asleep. And then, one day, when I was ready, I went into school and I went up to the chief bully and I punched him in the face, as hard as I could. And he fell on the ground and I kicked him where it hurts, you know?

Ollie nods.

And then your Uncle Bernie – he was really young – he came over and spat on him and he said, 'You touch my brother again and we'll kill you.'

And no one touched me again.

Pause.

Ollie D'you think *I* should learn to fight?

Katz Well . . . you *could*.

Ollie Would Grandpa teach me?

Beat.

Katz No. *I'd* teach you.

Pause.

Ollie Why do they call me a girl?

Katz puts his arm round the boy.

Katz Because . . . you're not rough. Because you're *gentle*. And 'gentle' is a wonderful thing to be.

Ollie Is gentle . . . like . . . *weak*?

Katz No. Not at all. Mummy's gentle and she's *strong*.

Ollie Mummy says I could change schools.

Katz I know. And you could. That's OK too. Because . . . me and your mum, all we want is for you to be *happy* . . . 's all we care about . . .

Ollie nods. Katz gazes at him.

Day you were born . . . I ran out the hospital . . . to smoke . . . to phone my dad . . . and . . . everything . . . (*Katz tries to remember.*) . . . it was a great day . . .

So . . . you want to get an ice cream?

Ollie No, thanks.

Katz Why not?

Ollie I just . . . don't like ice cream.

Katz's house. Night.

Jess Where were you?

Katz Driving. I drove . . . miles . . . out of town. Until I was lost. But I ignored the map. And I found my way home. Sorry, I should've phoned.

Jess Ollie had a fight, at school. He hit another boy in the face.

Beat.

Katz Good for him.

Jess No, *bad* for him. And bad for *you.*

Katz *Me?*

Jess He told me you told him to fight.

Katz I didn't *tell* him, I said it was an *option.*

Jess Well, it was really stupid of you.

Katz You think he should take it? Give in? Let them terrify him?

Jess I don't want him fighting.

Katz Nothing's worth having you didn't fight for.

Jess Says who? Your *father?* We're changing schools.

Katz That's right, turn him into a little *posh-boy.*

Jess You *know* he'll be happier. All our friends send their kids to private schools.

Katz All our friends are *hypocrites.*

Jess So let's join them. I'm sorry. No, I'm *not* sorry. It's *right.*

Katz (*glances up*) Sorry, mate.

Jess God's not a socialist.

Katz Well, he's not a fucking *Tory.*

Jess sits, picks up her book.

Oh, cheer up, misery's *my* job.

He prods her, tenderly. Jess looks at him.

Jess Could we have sex tonight?

Pause.

Katz Well, it's certainly an *option*.

Pause.

Jess You don't fancy me.

Katz Yes I do.

Jess If I was a *babe* you would.

Katz Babe, you're a babe. OK?

Katz kisses her. She strokes his face.

Jess Whatever it is you're *up to* . . . you *can* let me in on it.

Katz I'm just . . . scratching around, earning a crust . . . *living*. There's nothing . . . it's *nothing* . . .

Jess goes back to her book. Katz paces, stops.

What's a merkin?

Jess A pubic wig.

Beat.

Katz Who on God's earth needs a pubic wig?

Jess Actors wear them, for nude scenes.

Katz How d'you *know* these things?

Jess Because I'm cleverer than you.

Pause.

Katz What's the book?

Jess *Mansfield Park.*

Katz What did *she* know? What did that prissy little bonnet know about . . . digital television.

Jess She knew about *people*.

Katz Rural toffs with turdy hairdos. Where's the *anger* in Jane Austen?

Jess She makes *you* angry.

Katz Fucking Hampshire *madam*.

Jess You should read it.

Katz *I* can't *read*. I can read *contracts*.

Anything else, the words start *dancing*.

I'm a moron.

Katz looks at her.

I lost another client today . . .

Jess Oh no, I'm sorry, who?

Katz gestures 'doesn't matter'.

Tell me . . .

Katz Do you ever want to –

He fights the air, Jess looks at him.

No, you don't, you really don't.

One day, I swear, I will set fire to myself and run through the streets *wailing*.

Jess Why are you sparring?

Katz Specifically because I'm bored. Generally . . . because I'm bored.

Katz looks at her curled up in her armchair.

Your capacity for happiness can be very depressing.

Jess (*smiles*) Will you shut the fuck up and let me *read*?

Pause. Katz lights a cigarette, smiles to himself.

Katz For how much money would you play Russian Roulette?

Jess? Love of my life. How much?

Standard revolver, odds are *heavily* in your favour, come on . . . name your price.

Jess thinks, looks at him, curious.

Jess What's *your* price?

Katz Eh?

Jess What's your price?

Katz Five to one on? (*Thinks.*) You'd have to get involved for a cool thirty mill.

Jess You'd risk your life for thirty million pounds?

Katz Who wouldn't?

Jess Anyone who *valued* their life.

Pause.

Katz Yeah but I'd *win*. I'm not gonna *die*, I'm gonna *win*.

Jess You'd risk losing me and Ollie for thirty million quid?

Katz No, no. Of course I wouldn't.

Jess (*tough*) Then don't say you *would*.

   Silence.

Katz (*muses*) Never have to work again though . . .

Jess Why are you bored?

Katz Why are you content?

Jess Because everything I want and need is right here in this house. Why are you bored? You said, you were *bored*, specifically and generally. Does that include *me*?

Katz Nohh, not *you*, I'm not bored with *you*. I love *you*.

Jess And *I love you* but you often *bore* me. But I don't mind this occasional boredom . . . because . . . despite your many and varied flaws, I want to live my life with you.

Katz Well, ditto. Would you mind telling me what we're talking about?

Jess We're talking about our marriage.

Katz *I'm* not.

Jess Yes you are. *In your way.*

   Pause. Jess slowly raises her hands, presents them to Katz . . .

38

Choose a finger.

I'm thinking of *one*.

Pretend it's a bullet.

Katz Eh?

Jess If you pick the bullet, you pack your bags and leave tonight.

And you don't come back. Non-negotiable.

What do you *value*?

Really.

Katz And . . . were I to *avoid* your (can I say, entirely *fictitious*) bullet, what's my reward?

Jess You get to *keep* what you've already *got*. Me and your son.

Beat.

Katz It's a silly game.

Jess No it's not. It's a truth game.

Katz I mean, where's the . . . where's the . . . ?

Jess (*defeated*) Incentive . . . ?

Long silence. They look at each other.

Katz Your little finger. On your left hand.

Did I choose the bullet?

Jess There wasn't one.

Jess exits.

39

Katz's office. Day.

Nat I'm not a whore.

Katz Hey, Nat, no one said you *were*.

Nat I can't believe you want me to pose for a men's magazine.

Katz It's not *my* idea. It's the 'Pulse' publicist who *brought it up*, I said I'd run it *by* you.

Nat Well, please tell him 'no'.

Katz My pleasure, I'll do it now. (*He reaches for the phone.*)

Nat Whenever. What's *your* opinion?

Katz Oh, cheap, tacky, not your *bag*.

Nat Right. Thank you. Thank you.

Pause.

Katz Of course . . . if you *had* wanted to do it, I'd support that too.

Nat What . . . ?

Katz You've nothing to be *ashamed* of; we'd have full creative control with airbrush approval.

Nat You think I should get my tits out?

Katz No I Do Not. I'm saying, if you *did* – it would not be demeaning *per se*. It's a *style* magazine, it's not *porn*, they just want a *glimpse*. I'd *be* there, I'd make *sure*.

Nat Wh–wh–what's a *glimpse*?

Katz It's *this*, it's *nothing*. (*He puts his arms across his chest to demonstrate.*)

Nat *Why?*

Katz Because, *darling*, it gets you *noticed*, it *speeds* things up. Call me a dinosaur but you are an Attractive Woman. This Is The World. We Are *All* Whores. Do I think you should do it? *No.* Would it be 'good for your career'? (*Katz shrugs: 'Yes'.*) But you're not *going* to do it. In fact, I *forbid* you to do it.

Nat Howard . . . you *know* me – I *thought* you knew me?

Katz Hey, look, *listen*: Nat: *truth*? Bitter pill time? 'The Pulse' is not *Shakespeare*. None of us are winning *prizes* round here. We're not feeding the *starving*, love. We're stuck in the arsehole end of this business trying to breathe some clean air. You see what I'm saying?

Nat Yes . . . (*She looks at him, sadly.*) I wish . . . I wish I was brilliant . . . at something . . .

   Katz puts his arm round her.

Katz *Hey*, you *are*. You're a natural presenter. People *like* you, it's a *kind* of brilliance.

Nat It's banal. I'm banal. I'm *ashamed* of myself.

Katz Hey, don't go there. You're *cliente numero uno*, you're the real deal. Come on . . . 'fame', 'luxury', 'everyone loves you' – why shouldn't you *want* that? *I* would.

Nat (*nods*) Where does that *come* from?

Katz It's the world, don't blame yourself.

Nat You really think I should do it?

Katz We get *one life*, Nat. And it's like me: short and ugly. Sup From The Golden Cup If You *Can*.

Nat Bern would go mad. He gets jealous.

Katz Look – let's – let's *talk* about Bern. He's my brother, he's a fine, *fine* fellow. But for *you*, where you are *now* . . . is he . . . *appropriate*?

Nat I love him, Howard.

Katz 'Course you do, we *all* love Bernie. But . . . Nat . . . 'love' . . . (*Katz grimaces.*) *love* . . . I love *Jess* but sometimes you have to make a *sacrifice* in order to move *forward* and I don't regret it, 'cos now I'm *free* and she's well rid of me – look, this situation is not about me, or Bernie, it's about *clarity*, it's about what *you* truly *want*.

Nat I need to do some thinking.

Katz No problem.

Nat I really need to.

Katz Yes, indeed.

Nat I'm going to do some serious thinking.

West End bar. Night. Katz and Bernie, drinking. Loud music plays.

They shout to be heard the whole scene.

Bern Nat was right to leave you, you're a pimp, mate.

Katz Natalie *left* me, *Bernard*, 'cos *you* wanted her to, you ludicrous, possessive *tosser*.

Bern I'm CONFUSED – what is it, what the fuck is it you *do*?

Katz You know EXACTLY what I do.

Bern Doing the deals, spieling, shmoozing, kissing up celebrity arse.

Katz *Micro*-celebrity arse.

Bern The *size* of the arse is irrelevant, you're still *kissing* it. You *lie for a living*, mate. Does talking on the phone all day give you a big *chubby*?

Katz Something like that.

Bern 'Something like that', 'something like that' – you sanctimonious *titbag*.

Katz Yeah, yeah.

Bern Don't 'yeah yeah' me, you hate me, you *goblin*. You don't respect me.

Katz YES I DO.

Bern NO, don't *lie*, 'cos I'm pissed and potentially *violent*, don't *lie*, 'cos I'm off my huge, hairy *tits*.

Katz What a profoundly depressing conversation.

Bern You sold your soul so long ago you don't remember the *price*.

Pause.

Katz I'm not denying it.

Bern What?

Katz I'M NOT DENYING IT.

Bern THANK YOU. Thank you. Now we have a dialogue. 'The Wandering Jew' . . .

Katz Eh?

Bern Legend *of*. He took the piss out of Jesus Christ on the cross so God condemned him to wander for all eternity without the ability to die. 'A Homeless Jew Who Took The Piss'. Want another?

Bernie exits in the direction of the bar.

Katz's rented flat. West End. Jo, Norman and Ellie are sitting.

Katz stands. Ellie is drinking coffee, Katz, Jo and Norman with brandy.

Ellie So you like this place?

Katz It's an elephant's graveyard for single men.

Ellie Expensive too, I guess.

Katz Crippling, I'm gonna move out.

Ellie You wanna come and live at home?

Beat.

Katz Nahh, thanks for the offer. I'll find some hovel.

Jo Is it flat?

Katz Eh?

Jo Is it one of these new flat tellies?

Katz Yes.

Jo And *wide*? Your brother, the expert, says they've got to be flat and wide.

Katz It's flat and wide.

Pause.

Ellie Do you see more picture?

Katz Eh?

Ellie With the width?

Katz No.

Ellie Then tell me the point?

Silence.

Norm Is it a Sony?

Katz Yeah.

Jo *Sony*. They know what they're doing.

Norm They're making money.

Jo They're making bundles. *All* of them. (*to Katz*) You ever met a Japanese beggar? You ever *seen* a Japanese *shnorrer*?

Katz 'Course I have, in Tokyo.

Jo You? When?

Ellie Year before last, he went on business.

Beat.

Jo Did he send us a card?

Katz (*sighs*) Yeass.

Jo She keeps all your cards. In a shoe box. She's got it labelled with . . . what's that . . . ?

Ellie Dymo. (*to Katz*) You remember?

Katz (*smiles*) Yep.

Jo She's the last living Dymo-user in England.

You give him any money, the *shnorrer*?

Katz I gave him a yen or two.

Jo What d'he say?

Katz (*thinks*) 'Arigato'.

 Beat.

Jo Very courteous, the Japs.

Katz You've met them *all*, have you?

Jo Every single one. You helped him on his way – he'll be head of Sony now.

 Katz looks at his watch. The other three are looking at him. Katz raises his glass.

Katz Happy birthday, Norm.

Jo/Ellie Happy birthday.

Katz Any more for anyone?

Ellie No, we should be going . . . (*Ellie fetches their coats and talks briefly to Jo.*)

Norm (*to Katz*) Thank you for dinner, very kind of you.

Katz Look at you, what's the secret?

Norm The secret: every day is a birthday.

Katz That's it?

Norm Nothing more.

Katz 'Maharishi Norm.'

Norm I'm not joking. I know you think it's bullshit.

Ellie hands Norman his coat.

Ellie 'Night, Howard.

Katz (*kisses her*) 'Night. I'll see you out.

Ellie and Norman start to exit. Katz turns to Jo, still sitting on the sofa.

Jo Your mother wants me to talk to you.

Katz turns, Ellie and Norman have gone. Katz sighs.

We don't have to.

Katz *Thank you.*

Pause. Jo glances at Katz.

Jo Have you spoken to Jess?

Katz No.

Jo Do you think you should?

Katz *Please*, Dad? (*Katz sits with Jo.*) I think I'm gonna take up drinking.

They clink glasses.

Jo *Lechayim.*

Katz How's *your* troubles?

Jo It doesn't go away. Every day I see your mother, I feel this guilt.

Katz Hey, Mum's OK, you know? Have you seen her . . . May?

Jo I went to beg. Like a *meshuggener*. Broke my heart all over again.

Katz What's she like?

Jo She's . . . you know . . .

Jo looks at Katz.

You're tired. D'you want me to go?

Pause. Katz looks at him.

Katz I hit Ollie.

Beat.

Jo I heard.

Katz Smacked him. (*Katz gestures 'a tiny cuff'.*) Last week. I hit my boy. Nothing worse in the world.

Jo What can I say?

Katz Think he'll forgive me . . . ?

Jo Do you forgive *me*?

Katz 'Course.

Jo So . . . ?

Katz I was a little shitface, I deserved it, *he's* sensitive.

Jo You were sensitive. There's no excuse.

Jo swigs his drink. Thinks. Smiles to himself.

Jo Do you remember . . . when you were a boy . . . I told you about your *pippik*?

Katz shakes his head.

How could you forget?

I told you that before you were born, you were on a giant conveyor belt and you passed before God, because he always inspects the babies; and the ones who are good to be born, God puts his finger in their bellies. And so your belly button *is* . . .

Katz (*softly*) 'The Fingerprint of God' . . . I remember now . . .

Jo It's not true. I lied.

Katz (*smiles*) There's no Fingerprint of God?

Jo I'm not even sure there's a God to fingerprint . . .

Katz No . . .?

Jo I dunno . . . what do *I* know . . .? Everything is wilderness.

Silence.

When she asks, tell her I gave you a talking?

Katz Yeah.

Jo Help me up?

Katz pulls Jo up from the sofa. He helps him put on his coat.

Katz I'll call you a cab.

Jo Nahh, save your money.

Katz I'll put it on the company.

Jo Nahh, I like to walk. Do a little thinking, it's not far.

Katz It's *miles*.

Jo So I'll do a *lot* of thinking.

They hug.

Don't go ruining your life, uh? Living in hovels, all alone.

Katz You be careful out there.

Jo Who's gonna mug an old Jew with no money?

Katz helps Jo with his gloves and scarf.

Katz I dunno; some *junkie*, some *thief*, some 'Care in the Community' *nutcase*.

Jo (*smiles*) Always thinking the worst . . .

Katz Damn right.

Jo Always on the attack . . .

Katz Gotta survive.

Jo So what does this do for your soul?

Katz Never had one.

Jo Tell me . . .

Katz Dad, we're pissed –

Jo Tell me . . .

Katz – and it's *late*.

Jo You were a good boy, you were a *passionate* soul. And *now*? It's my fault, I taught you badly.

Katz The mess I'm in, is not your fault. Goodnight.

Jo Don't – don't *dismiss* me, I'm trying to talk to you. It's easy to be cynical, much harder to *care*.

Katz Understood.

Jo Everyone blames the government.

Katz You *what*?

Jo People forget how sick the others were.

Katz (*bundling him out*) Whatever.

Jo These are better but everybody –

Katz They're the *same*, Dad.

Jo *No*, they're *not* the same. These care more.

Katz They don't give a toss.

Jo Yes they do. Don't be lazy in your thoughts. It takes a long time to change anything. *Anything*. Tiny steps. They'll do it.

Katz You're living in a fantasy world.

Jo (*snaps*) Don't tell me where I'm living. What did *you* do? Uh? What did *you* ever do?

Katz Hey?

Jo *Tell me*. They're out there *shlepping* for their country, and *you*? You're shovelling shit into this world.

Katz (*angry*) You know what *I* did? I provided for my family. I worked my balls off for my son and my wife. That's what *I* did.

Jo We *all* do that. That's the *deal*, son. We go out there to *provide* so we can come back to *kindness*. The job is to *cope*, to do your *duty*. Not to *walk away*. Suffer by all means but don't *walk away*. We *all* earn a living.

Katz Yeah? How *much* of a living? Holidays? Good school? *Money*. Don't tell *me* where I went wrong – look at *yourself*.

   Silence.

I didn't mean that.

Jo Is this how you feel?

Katz No . . .

Jo (*softly*) You had holidays . . .

Katz I'm not saying we didn't.

Jo I always *encouraged* you . . .

Katz I know . . .

Jo I don't have your brains. I don't have your sick talent for money.

I'm going now . . .

Katz Dad . . .

Jo I'm gonna go . . .

Katz Dad . . . *Dad*, you're not listening . . .

Jo I don't need to *listen*. I *heard*. (*Jo moves to exit.*) You've never believed anything, son.

So you don't know who you are.

And I say this with love.

As Jo exits, Katz finds himself with Bernie, by the river, at night.

Bern You reckon we go anywhere?

Katz Nahh . . .

Bern Be nice to, though. Heaven.

Katz I don't think Yiddlers go *anywhere*. I think we go to God but God is . . . *everywhere* so . . . (*Looks up.*) I'm a bad Jew.

Bern Pig-ignorant?

Katz (*smiles*) We should go to *shul*. You wanna go to *shul* sometime?

Bern (*shrugs*) Could do . . .

Katz Saturday?

Bern We're at home.

Katz *Shul*'s in the *morning*, you *shmok*, go to the game after.

Bern Yeah, I'll get back to you.

Katz (*smiles*) How's Nat?

Bern Yeah, good, really good. (*He glances at Katz.*) I think she's gonna leave me.

Katz Why?

Bern We go to these parties and openings, meet these people, I've got nothing to *say*, H. I'm standing there like a s*chlemiel*, I tell 'em I'm a *barber,* they're like . . . (*He grimaces.*) I'm out of me depth.

Katz She loves you *because* you're out of your depth.

Bern You reckon?

Katz Hang in there, you'll be alright.

Bern Spend your whole life waiting for someone. And then she *comes* . . . spend your whole life waiting for her to *go*.

How's *your* troubles?

Katz Nahh . . .

Bern You're insane. Go back to her.

Katz She's seeing someone.

Bern It's serious?

Katz nods.

Katz 'Bernie, Bernie, Bern.' What you gonna do with the shop?

Bern Keep at it, I've got a few ideas . . .

Katz Good for you.

Bern Wanna job?

Katz No ta.

They look at each other. Nod.

Katz takes two white yarmulkes from his pocket. He offers Bern the choice. Bern puts one on, Katz the other.

Bern removes an urn from a grey plastic bag (the one Katz has at the beginning of the play).

They contemplate the urn.

Bern He was a good man.

Katz He was a *mensh*.

Bern And a bastard.

Katz Yes . . .

Bern offers the urn to Katz.

Bern You wanna do this?

Katz You do it, if you want . . .

Bern He'd've wanted *you* to do it.

Katz No . . .

Bern He *would*.

Pause.

Katz We weren't speaking. When he died. Did he tell you?

Bern No . . .

Katz We had a row. I hurt him, Bern . . .

Bern (*softly*) Go on . . .

Bern passes the urn to Katz. Katz unscrews the lid.

Katz I can't look . . .

Katz looks inside the urn, briefly.

A man drops down dead. What does it *mean*?

Bern If there *is* a God, he's *unjust*. That's what it means.

Katz Don't say that.

Bern It's true.

Katz Maybe it *is* but –

Bern Always *right*, yeah?

Katz Hey?

Bern grunts an apology. Katz takes out a prayer book.

I'm gonna say Kaddish.

Bern Yeah?

Katz I learnt it . . .

Bern Well, so did *I* . . .

Katz Did you . . . ?

Bern Dad asked me to . . .

Katz Did he . . . ?

Bern 'Course he fucking didn't, get on with it.

Katz smiles. They crouch low to the water.

Katz You do it. I want you to. Please.

Bern nods, takes the urn and starts to scatter the ashes as Katz begins to say Kaddish for their father.

A park. Day. May (played by 'Ellie') enters.

May This must be strange for you, so thank you.

Katz hands her a shoe-box.

May I?

Katz Of course, they're yours.

May sits, opens the box. It contains letters. May
flicks through them. Katz watches her.

May Did you read them?

Katz No. Some of them. I'm sorry.

May Would you . . . like to read his?

She gestures to her bag. Katz shakes his head.

Katz No. Thank you. Who did you marry?

May (*slight smile*) My ex-husband.

I don't want to die alone. It's a weakness.

I've . . . I'm not a good person . . . I've made many
mistakes in my life.

When Joseph – when your father died . . . I believed
this was something *waiting* for me . . . a punishment.

Katz You believe in God?

May Yes.

Katz What does he do for you?

May He comforts me. Do you believe?

Katz Sometimes. (*Shrugs.*) At night, in bed, when
every little ache makes me feel like I'm dying . . .
I pray to God.

May You're quite like your father, if you don't mind
me saying.

Katz Did he ever talk about me?

May Often. He was very proud. You're in 'entertain-
ment', aren't you?

Katz nods. Pause.

How's your mother?

Katz looks at her, confused momentarily.

Katz She's . . . I think . . . people can lose the will to live, you know?

Pause.

May Would she . . . would you mind – would it *help* if . . . if I wrote to her, to *explain* . . . ?

Katz No. *No.* It would not *help*.

Are you insane? What d'you *want* from us?

May I didn't mean –

Katz I thought I might find someone who knows what *guilt* is.

You *destroyed* him, now live with it, you *Christian*.

And you know something else? YOU CAN'T EVEN SPELL.

Katz's office. Late afternoon. Greg, Katz's boss, is distributing coffees from a cardboard tray. Tina, another agent, sits on the sofa. (Greg to be played by 'Bern', Tina to be played by 'Jess'.)

Greg Grande Cappuccino for *Howard*.

Katz Thanks, Greg.

Greg Tall Skinny Latte for *Tina*.

Tina Thanks, Greg.

Greg Espresso Machiatto *per me*.

Tina You need a degree to buy this stuff!

Katz feigns amusement. The phone rings.

Katz Sorry, I'm expecting a –

Greg waves that it's 'OK'.

(*in phone*) Yes. No. Of course it's in *writing*. It's in legally binding *lawyer* writing, *pal*. Hey, *screw* the residuals. (*to Greg*) Sorry. (*in phone*) Can – can we talk about this tomorrow? I'm in a meeting. Listen, you dummy, a contract's a contract . . . oh yeah? Go swivel. (*He slams the phone down.*) Little tin-pot independents. *Lunatics*.

Greg Mmm . . .

Beat. Katz grabs the phone.

Katz Sorry. (*in phone*) *Rach*? Will you call 'shitface' and tell him – tell him it's 'in hand'. And no more calls. Thanks. (*to Greg and Tina*) Sorry.

Beat.

Tina Howard, how are you feeling?

Katz Are you sacking me?

Greg No! NO! Why? *Should* we?

Greg and Tina laugh a little.

Katz You are, aren't you?

Tina No. *Really*. We value you *enormously*.

Katz What've I *done*?

Greg Howard. Relax. OK? *Relax*.

Beat.

Katz Will you just *do* it?

Greg (*slight loss of temper*) Christ, he's so *tense*. Howard. *Please*.

Now . . . now . . . *now* . . . Tina.

Tina We . . . *feel* . . . that you aren't entirely happy. And we want you to *be* happy. We *feel* that some time off would be . . . no bad thing. And *then*, we could all assess . . . where we *are*.

Greg Mmm.

Katz Hey, I'm *fine*. I've had, as you know, some personal stuff but I'm *fine*. I like it here. I . . . (*to Tina*) Hey, we *all* get depressed and . . . my dad *died*. I admit that sometimes I don't *handle* things as I should but –

Greg Howard, do you know how many assistants you've been through? This year alone? *Twelve*. It's *June*.

Katz *Rachel* stays.

Tina (*sharp*) Rachel's a saint.

Katz Assistants are young and ambitious, they *move on*, it's *natural*.

Greg Come *on*.

Katz (*to Greg*) Hey, at least I don't *fuck* 'em.

Greg (*to Tina*) See?

Tina Howard –

Katz Do you know how much commission I bring in? I'm doing all right – and I'm not saying I'm so *great* or anything but – *Jesus* – I look after all the flotsam and jetsam nobody *wants*: the weather girls and the chefs and the gardeners and the game-show winners, the singers who want to act and the actors who want to sing, strange blonde ladies with one name. I've got a client in the *Scrubs* – I visit him once a month. Alcoholics, cokeheads, perverts, the lost and the mad – 'Sling 'em down the corridor to Howard, he'll mop up.' Hideous, *hideous* egos – all of them – *monsters* – kicking and screaming for their 'fifteen minutes' – and on top of that I'm brown-nosing the press and sucking up to ad-men and gobbling off the broadcasters and milking the tits of every vicious, fame-fucking publicist in London – it's *Sodom* and *Gomorrah* out there – but without the *scenery* – and I'm squelching around in this . . . *this infantile morass,* holding the clients' hands and wiping their chins through every piddling 'crisis' in their so-called 'lives' and I'm doing this 24/7 for YOU. I am *Juggling Turds* Every Day Of My *Life* so that this *noble* agency can look after the so called 'artists' who don't actually earn us enough *commission* to PAY THE RENT ON THE OFFICE.

Greg Is that a respectful way to refer to your clients?

Katz I *love* my clients. I *totally* respect them – I *understand* them: their *desperation* and their sense of . . . *failure.* Me and my clients are very happy, thank you. (*Katz cradles his Rolodex.*)

Tina Well . . .

Katz *What*?

Tina A number *have* been leaving.

Katz And a number *have* been joining.

Greg *Vastly unequal* numbers: Natalie North –

Katz That was for personal reasons.

Greg She still *left*. There are others – you let Ricky Barnes walk straight out of here.

Katz He's a prick, you *know* that.

Greg You told Melanie Dunn she'd had plastic surgery for Christ's sake.

Katz (*explodes*) She HAS – she *needed* to be told, for her CAREER.

Greg Howard. It's not just the clients, it's *everything*: your manner, your *expenses*, your – you've destroyed *three* telephones this *week*. All we are saying – and this is a *company* decision – not just *me*, not just Tina, *all* of us, we're saying: Take Some Time. Think. Consider. Ponder. And then we'll discuss.

Katz (*desperately*) Oh . . . oh . . . *please*. Come on. I've been here *for ever*. I grew up here. I *belong* here. I'm not gonna be able to . . . once I'm out of that door . . . you *know* what happens. *Please*. Greg? Don't . . . don't humiliate me . . . *please*?

Greg It's a company decision. We're *sorry*. We can't sustain this . . . *instability*. You've always been something of a – and we *like* you for this – a loose cannon, but quite honestly, your behaviour, recently, has been totally unacceptable. We . . . actually, we think you should seek some . . . professional help. We're sorry.

Silence.

Katz You know something, *Greg*. I'd call you a cunt if I could – but I *can't*. Because you're not even a cunt. You don't even *make it* to *cunt*. Not even *wanker*. You're just a *tit*. In fact, you're a *tit's tit*.

Greg starts to exit. Katz shouts after him.

And don't bother to say, 'Clear Your Desk' like some boss in a *film* – 'cos I QUIT. And I don't want a *thing* from you: I don't want the *car*, I don't want your *pity*, and I don't want your MONEY. So why don't *you* 'clear my desk'?

Tina exits.

Both of you. AND ALL OF YOU OUT THERE.

I hated every single second in this stinking job.

In fact, *thank you*.

Thank you for giving me the chance to SAVE MY LIFE.

Blackout.

Act Two

Hotel room. Night.

Katz sits, thinking.

A Bell Boy (played by 'Robin') enters in uniform.

He carries a suitcase.

Bell Boy Good evening, Sir. (*He puts the suitcase down.*) Have you stayed with us before, Sir?
Sir?

   Katz shakes his head.

Shall I show you how the air-conditioning works?
Sir?

Katz Do you like working here?

Bell Boy Yes, Sir.

Katz Do you resent the guests?

Bell Boy Sir . . .?

Katz One night in this room might cost as much as you earn in a week. You don't resent that?

Bell Boy No, Sir.

Katz Why not?

Bell Boy It's not my job. My job is to *serve* the guests, not to resent them, Sir.

Katz stands.

Katz Do you want to stay in the hotel business?

Bell Boy I'd like to, if I can.

Katz Why?

Bell Boy Sir?

Katz *Why?*

Bell Boy I like it, Sir. The people who work here are . . . decent.

Will that be all, Sir?

Katz My parents . . . spent their wedding night in this hotel.

I might've been *conceived* in this room.

Where were *you* conceived?

Beat.

Bell Boy I don't know, Sir. Will that be all, Sir?

Katz Here. (*He gives the Bell Boy a £50 note.*)

Bell Boy Thank you, Sir. Very generous.

Katz Very *rich*. You know what's wrong with this country?

Bell Boy No, Sir.

Katz *You and me*. The money won't make you *belong*. They don't *want* you to belong. They want you to serve them.

Beat.

Bell Boy Will that be all, Sir?

Katz Yes. You're *free*. Go back to the . . . *pantry* . . . and tell your decent friends about the lunatic in 243.

Bell Boy Sir.

Katz looks at the Bell Boy, speaks passionately:

Katz Take some advice: go and *live*, do something you *love*.

Bell Boy Yes, Sir.

Katz Will you get my case, please?

Bell Boy Sir?

Katz I'm checking out.

Bell Boy Yes, Sir. (*The Bell Boy collects the suitcase, makes to exit.*)

Katz Can you recommend a real shit-hole? Somewhere with hookers and lice.

Bell Boy I think you'd be wanting King's Cross, Sir.

Katz Of course.

Bell Boy Goodnight, Sir.

Katz Goodnight.

As the Bell Boy is exiting Mr Lord (played by 'Jo') enters with a breakfast tray. He moves slowly.

Katz is now in a shabby bed-and-breakfast hotel.

Mr Lord Breakfast. (*He hands the tray to Katz, points to the plate.*) Broke your egg. (*He starts to exit.*)

Katz Is that an apology?

Mr Lord No. It's a *fact*.

Katz (*peers at the egg*) I don't want it.

Mr Lord returns and, grudgingly, collects the tray.

Mr Lord You're a week behind with the rent.

Katz Why's there no Bible in here?

Mr Lord They never came. The Gideons. (*Mr Lord starts to exit.*)

Katz They go *everywhere*.

Mr Lord turns, thinks, finally admits:

Mr Lord Someone stole it.

Katz Could I borrow a Bible, from another room? Please.

Mr Lord (*suspiciously*) What d'you want it for?

Katz I want to read it.

Mr Lord Bible, no. Rent, yes.

Katz What's it like, being *you*?

Mr Lord (*exiting*) It is abysmal.

A masseuse, Cheryl, enters (played by 'Natalie'). She wears a white uniform, like a hygienist, but with trainers.

Cheryl I'll come back. (*She hands Katz a towel.*)

Katz I don't want a massage.

Cheryl thinks.

Cheryl OK. Can you put this on? (*She produces a condom from her top pocket. Gives it to Katz.*)

Katz Will you kiss me?

Cheryl I don't kiss.

Katz But you'll fuck me?

Cheryl Yeh.

Katz It's adolescence in reverse!

    Cheryl looks at him, no expression.

What else d'you do?

Cheryl French and hand relief.

Katz No. When you're away from *here*.

Cheryl Nothing. I look after my daughter.

Katz Ahh, what's her name?

Cheryl D'you want something or what?

    Beat.

Katz What's 'French'?

Cheryl Oral.

Katz OK. I'll have French. How much?

Cheryl Twenny-five. (*Gestures to condom.*) Will you put that on. Please.

Katz You want me to wear this for a *blow job*?

Cheryl *Yeh.*

    Katz takes down his trousers . . .

Katz Oh . . .

Cheryl *What?*

Katz I can't *get* it on just now . . .

Cheryl Not my problem.

Katz It *is*, actually.

Cheryl You shoulda had the massage then, shouldn't ya?

Katz Please?

Cheryl rubs his crotch, Katz gazes at her.

Cheryl Alright?

Katz (*softly*) Yes. Thank you. That's nice. You're very nice.

Cheryl So are you. Now put the rubber on, yeh? (*Cheryl stops rubbing him, wipes her hand on the towel.*)

Katz I . . . would you mind . . . ?

Katz gestures, Cheryl turns her back.

Thanks, it's just . . .

Cheryl Yeah, yeah.

Katz (*snaps*) Can't you just *pretend* to be a 'tart with a heart'?

Cheryl I – don't – *do* – *chat*. Alright?

Katz Yeah, well I don't *do* erection. (*Katz pulls his trousers up.*)

Cheryl Is that it then?

Katz Yeah, that's it. This is really depressing, *Cheryl*. Because we're *human beings*. And it's a beautiful Sunday afternoon out there . . . and God has bestowed upon us this . . . this *thing* called *life*. And it's a wonderful . . . *offering*. SO WHY DOESN'T IT FEEL LIKE ONE?

Night. An alley. Martin and Felix approach Katz.

Martin You the guy who wants something? Are you the man who's been . . . *inquiring*?

Katz Yes.

Martin OK.

Pause.

Katz Who are you?

Martin Who d'you know?

Katz I don't understand.

Martin Who – do – you – *know*?

Katz I don't know anyone.

Martin Why are you *here*?

Katz In the pub, someone said –

Martin *Someone* said? No, no, no – *you* said.

Katz Yes. I'm sorry.

Martin Don't be *sorry*. What d'you want?

Katz I wanna buy a gun.

Martin Hey, hey, hey, *shhh*.

Katz (*whispers*) I wanna buy a piece.

Martin A *piece* . . .

Katz A gun.

Martin What for, Mr Bond?

Katz That's my business.

Martin You want it or not?

Katz It's for someone I know.

Martin Who's *he*?

Katz He's a friend, he's a guy I know.

Martin What's his name?

Katz Howard.

Martin What's he want it for?

Katz He wants to – I don't *know* what he wants it for. Maybe to –

Martin Yeah, yeah, yeah. So what'you looking for?

Katz I really *want* a revolver. Do you have any revolvers?

Martin 'Course we do.

Beat.

Katz How much?

Martin How much d'you *think*?

Katz Er . . . three hundred?

Felix sniggers.

You see . . . I'm naive, so why don't you *tell me*.

Martin (*to Felix*) Be *still*. (*to Katz*) Don't mind him, he's deaf.

Katz He's *death*?

Martin *Deaf*, deaf – can't hear. (*to Felix*) CAN YA? (*to Katz*) How d'you fancy a *Russian*?

Katz Russian . . .? Will it work?

Martin Trust me.

Beat.

Katz How much?

Martin You wanna rent it or you wanna own it?

Katz Eh?

Martin *Rent* it: use it, bring it back. Like a car. Or a wedding suit.

Katz Hmm . . .

Martin Sounds like you wanna *own* it. That's gonna be dear. (*He considers.*) It's gonna be a grand.

Katz A *grand*?

Martin It's an imported item. This is the *price*.

Katz I've got eight hundred . . .

Martin You got the cash on you?

Katz Yeah, have *you* got the –

Martin I don't have nothing, *Howard*. I'm like you, the 'middle man'. You get it later. Somewhere else.

Katz And . . . can I . . . inspect it? Before I buy it?

Martin Wot, like 'Antiques Roadshow'? You think I'm gonna sell you somefin' broken?

Katz No, but –

Martin What?

Katz I don't wanna buy a starter pistol.

Martin D'you *ask* for a starter pistol?

Katz No.

Martin So I'm not selling you one. You *want* a starter pistol?

Katz No.

Martin You wanna start a horse race or a swimming race?

Katz No.

Martin So don't be *naive*.

   Beat.

Katz And . . . I'll need bullets.

Martin Yeah, you *might*.

Katz I . . . assume they're included.

Martin Yeah, like batteries.

Katz I don't mind you ripping me off. And I don't mind that it's necessary for you to humiliate me. And

I'm not unaware of the pleasure it brings. But I *want* this. And I will do what it takes to acquire it. So don't sell me some piece of shit which doesn't work, yeah?

Pause.

Martin Why don't you give me your money?

Silence

Katz Eh?

Martin There's no gun. There's just you and us and your money.

Beat.

Katz I can't give you my money. It's all I've got.

Martin It's all we want. Please.

Katz looks at Felix. Felix has his hands in his coat pockets. He moves one hand, suggesting a weapon. Katz, scared, turns to Martin.

Katz Is a 'knife' a 'blade'?

Martin No, Sir. A knife is a knife.

Katz takes out an envelope full of cash, hands it to Martin.

Katz You're a pro. I respect that.

Martin Always here.

Martin exits. Felix stares at Katz.

Katz What are *you* looking at?

Felix Nothing.

74

Felix takes his hands out his pockets. Katz flinches.

Felix smiles. Felix exits.

Another day. Street. Katz slowly sinks to his knees.
He thinks. Then he slowly raises his hand to beg.
He speaks softly, to himself.

Katz Am I a beggar?

Or just . . . pretending to beg?

I've got a little money.

So what am I begging for?

He remembers something . . .

'Arigato.'

Another day. Katz sits with a piece of chalk,
drawing on the ground. A boy (played by 'Ollie')
approaches, watches him. Katz glances up.

Boy What's that?

Katz It's going to be a map. A map of all the places
I've ever been.

The boy looks at the map. Katz continues to draw.

Boy Where's *here*?

Katz I'm not up to here yet.

Katz looks at the boy.

What's your name?

The boy's mother sees him talking to Katz.

Mother John, come here.

The boy goes to her. Turns back to look at Katz.

Don't stare at him.

They exit.

Another day. A single chord. Distant ukulele. Quick fade down to follow spot on Katz. He sings, slowly, softly, remembering . . . 'Leaning on a Lamp-Post'.

Katz
Leaning on a lamp . . .
Maybe you think I look a tramp . . .
Or you may think I'm hanging round to steal a car . . .
But no, I'm not a crook,
And if you think that's what I look,
I'll tell you why I'm here and what my motives are . . .

I'm leaning on a lamp-post at the corner of the street,
In case a certain little lady comes by,
Oh me, oh my, I hope the little lady comes by . . .

He does a strange little dance of joy as the lights snap up . . .

Norm Howard . . .

A laundrette. Day.

Norman appears with a basket of washing. Katz goes to him. Norman's hands are bandaged.

Katz Let me help you . . .

Katz begins to sort socks and underwear.

Sometimes I wanna *destroy*, everything.

76

Norm The world?

Katz Yeah, but I'd start with 'Ingerlund'.

Norm Let me know when you do, I'll go on my holidays.

Pause.

Katz Hey, Norm. Why don't I kill 'em?

Norm Who?

Katz These . . . guys, who cut you.

Norm They're not 'guys', they're *kids*. With nothing to do.

Katz They've got things to do.

Norm They didn't *cut* me, don't blow it up, they pushed me and I fell.

Katz So let's teach 'em a lesson. It's a *cause*.

Norm Ahh, they're just ignorant.

Katz And racist?

Norm *Because* they are ignorant. Blame the education.

Katz No! *Fuck* that. Blame *them*. Blame *them* for what they did.

Norm Maybe. But killing is not necessary here.

Katz So what are you gonna do when they do it again?

Pause.

Norm They *won't* do it again.

Katz Well, you let me know if they *do*.

Norm Yeah. I'll call you on the 'bat-phone'.

Beat.

Katz 'Every day's a birthday', huh?

Norm Have to believe it.

Katz (*snaps*) *Why?* Why don't you accept the evidence *against*?

Norm (*angry*) And why don't *you* look in the mirror. And why don't *you* learn a little *humility*. And why don't *you* visit your *mother* and your *son*. That's what *I* believe. You're wasting your life, Howard.

Pause. Katz holds up a pair of absurd boxer shorts.

Katz You *wear* these?

Norm Yeah. What's wrong with them?

Beat.

Katz Thanks for seeing me, Norm. How's my brother?

Norm I thought you knew?

Katz I don't know anything, *what*?

Norman shrugs.

Norm Doesn't matter.

Katz *Tell* me . . .

Bern is sweeping up in the barber shop.

Bern Hey, look who's here! Welcome to the world.

Bern opens his arms, Katz stays still.

Katz Norman just told me you sacked him.

Pause.

Bern Yeah.

Katz Why?

Bern 'Cos . . . he doesn't fit in.

Katz He says you're doing building work.

Bern Modernisation.

Katz He's worked here *for ever*. He's *family*. He's Ollie's *godfather*.

Bern I gave him some dough. He's alright.

Katz What the fuck is 'modernisation'?

Bern *Don't* – don't worry about it – I was gonna tell you when I saw you – I just haven't seen you. We'll keep the *name* . . .

Katz What about the customers? The regulars?

Bern They don't come. Not without Dad. We need *new* customers. Whole area's going mad. It's a gold mine, H. I've got a bank loan, investors – give us a *break*. Nat's gonna help, she's got a good eye, she's arty – she'll get us a bit of press – strip it back to the brickwork, wooden floor, it'll *work*.

Katz looks at Bern. Silence.

Katz He would weep. You *know* he would.

Bern I don't know that.

Katz Yeah you do.

Bern I *worked* with Dad. Every day. Just 'cos you worshipped him, doesn't mean you *knew* him. This is *mine*.

Katz You can't sack him, Bern.

Bern Yeah I can.

Katz *Why?*

Bern He's not even good at the job.

Katz *Even?*

Bern He's no good at the job.

Katz He's alright.

Bern I don't want 'alright'. He's the wrong profile.

Katz *Profile?* Oh, you bastard.

Bern Kids don't want some old geezer cutting their hair.

Katz Some *foreign* geezer?

Bern Whatever.

Katz (*passionately*) We're *Jews*, Bern. We're *Jews*, we're fucking *Yids*.

Bern So?

Katz So we're not racists. So we're not gonna live in hatred. And we believe in the family. And we believe in *justice*.

Bern Don't come in 'ere like fuckin' *Topol*. Piss off.

Katz Come on, Bern, give him his job back. Come on, *please*.

Bern (*casually*) Sorry, mate. (*Bern starts sweeping again.*)

Katz Don't call me 'mate', I'm your brother.

Bern (*turns*) So *be* one. Be on my side. Just *once*.

   Pause.

Katz How d'you think Dad managed to pay you three-fifty a week?

Bern I *worked* for it.

Katz Norm was on three, top whack.

Bern So?

Katz So where did the money come from? To pay you *more*?

Bern Dad *gave* it to me.

Katz Eh?

Bern Dad paid me extra because I was his *son*. What's wrong with that?

Katz Nothing. He loved you. And he wanted you to feel like a *Big Man*. So he paid you more money, more than he could afford. And the *money* . . . came from *me*. *Fifteen* years I paid you. So don't you change a thing. And you give this man – this man we've known *all our lives*, you give him his job and you be a good man.

Pause.

Bern Why d'you tell me? Why d'you have to tell me?

Katz 'Cos you're a fucking *spiv*. 'Cos you've got no values.

Bern I've got values. Here's my *values*.

Bern hits Katz. Katz falls to the floor. Bern kicks him.

Don't *preach* to *me*. Don't *preach* to *me*, you spoilt, selfish CUNT.

Bern spits on him. Exits.

Katz lies on the ground, whimpering.

He sees something offstage, starts to cry . . . Jo enters, wearing his old barber's jacket. He holds Katz.

Jo Shh . . . shh . . . son . . . shh . . .

Katz I'm a gonner, Dad. I'm going crazy . . .

I'm scared . . . I don't know how to *be* . . . tell me what to do . . .

Jo Go back. Go back to your life.

Jo starts to exit.

Katz I said Kaddish for you.

Jo I know. Thank you.

Katz *Somewhere* . . . there's gotta be *someone* who knows what's going on . . .

Does *God*? Have you met him?

Jo (*shrugs*) No.

I'm nowhere near, son.

Nowhere near.

Jo exits.

Lobby of Katz's old office. A Security Guard stands in the background. Katz waits, dishevelled, trying to smarten up.

Katz Excuse me, Sir. How do I look?

Guard How d'you *want* to look?

Katz Respectable.

Guard You look it.

Katz Yeah? Wish me luck . . .?

Guard Good luck.

Marcia appears.

Marcia Mr Katz, Tina's on the phone. She'll be down soon. Can I get you anything?

Katz (*stares*) Do I *know* you?

Marcia (*coolly*) I was your assistant. Briefly. Marcia. Can I get you anything?

Katz Give us a smile?

Marcia Tina's on her way.

Tina enters, sees Katz, immediately gestures for Marcia to stay.

Tina Howard . . .

Katz It's decent of you to see me, I appreciate and respect it. Have you done something with your hair?

Tina shakes her head.

Well, you're looking good. Are we going upstairs?

Tina Here's fine.

Katz OK . . . erm, I've taken some time off, as you suggested, and I've thought about *things* – and you were absolutely right about needing to 'ponder' so I've spent some time 'pondering' and you know what I discovered: I have *no hidden depths*, right *here* is *exactly* where I belong. I'm *showbiz* – that's the *point* of me! How's Greg?

Tina He's at lunch.

Katz (*softly*) Lunch. Lovely. Where's he gone?

Tina The usual.

Katz Yeah, *'course*. So, I was thinking maybe you might let me – I don't think I should *look after* anyone but I could answer the phone, take messages, make coffee, update the old . . . erm . . . erm . . .

He mimes, slowly at first and then with increasing desperation.

What is it?

Pause.

Marcia Rolodex.

Katz *That's* the feller, thank you. I mean, I *know this business*.

Tina Well . . . I'll talk to Greg.

Katz Great. You'll talk to him?

Tina Yes.

Katz Thank you, Tina.

Tina It's a pleasure. I'm just popping out to get a sandwich so why don't you – (*She tries to usher him to the exit.*)

Katz What d'you think he'll say?

Tina As soon as I've spoken to him, I'll let you know.

Katz Thank you. (*He kisses Tina.*) Nice seeing you again, Marcia.

    Katz picks up his grey plastic bag to come with Tina. Bottles clank.

Tina Howard. Can I give you this? (*She hands him a card from her purse.*) It's the name and number of my therapist. She's really nice. Why don't you call her?

Katz Eh?

Tina Call her, have a chat.

Katz (*realises*) Oh . . . oh . . . I get it . . . (*He smacks his forehead, angry at himself.*) I wanna see *Greg*.

Tina He's at lunch, Howard.

Katz 'Course he is. 'Course he is. (*Katz tries to get into the office area.*)

Marcia (*to Guard*) Do something, you stupid man.

Katz Where's Greg? I wanna see Greg NOW.

Marcia He's *there*.

Greg has entered with Ricky Barnes. Tina glances at Greg: 'trouble'.

Katz goes on one knee.

Katz Greg. The noble Greg. Nice lunch? Fine wines quaffed?

Greg Er . . . *yes*, thank you . . .

Katz You back in the fold, Ricky?

Ricky Yeah.

Katz (*to Greg*) Aren't you a clever poacher? You old dog! Woof woof! This is *opportune*, 'cos me and T were just negotiating my *own* return . . . so . . . I know *him*, he knows *me*, how about I *assist* young Ricky? Deal with all your . . . fan mail. What d'you say? Greg?

Greg Er . . . well . . . it's a *thought* . . . Ricky?

Ricky I've got an assistant.

Katz (*pleads*) Have another one, you can never have *too many*. Think about it?

Beat.

Ricky I've thought about it, Howard, and . . . I've come to the conclusion that your bubble's burst. Know what I mean?

Greg (*laughs nervously*) Er . . . 'ouch'. Ha ha. Sorry, Howard.

Freeze. Katz looks at them as . . .

A Hospital Orderly wheels in Katz's mother, Ellie. The previous scene 'disappears'.

Orderly Mr Katz . . .

Katz Thank you.

Mum. It's Howard.

Ellie Yes.

Katz Do you know me? I'm your son.

Ellie Howard.

Katz Yes. I brought you a photo. This is me. And Bernie. Look, when we were small. We're brothers. We're your sons. And the woman, there, is you. And this is Dad. This is your husband. Jo. Do you remember Jo?

Beat.

Ellie There was a bee.

Katz A bee . . . ?

Ellie It came in through the window.

I could see the wings. They moved so slowly.

It didn't sting me.

Pause.

Katz I'm sorry I never saw you. I've been away. I went to the jungle. Do you remember? But I'm coming back now, I'm here for you now . . .

Ellie It flew away.

Katz puts the photo in her hand.

87

Katz Do you want this?

Ellie Yes.

Katz You want this?

Ellie It was going somewhere hot.

Katz The bee?

Ellie It was small but big for a bee.

Katz Yes.

Ellie Big fat bee.

Katz Big fat bumblebee.

Ellie It didn't sting me.

Katz No.

Ellie I stroked it.

He holds her hand. Takes the photo, puts it in his pocket. The Orderly wheels her away.

Katz's House. Early morning.

Katz is asleep on the sofa. Ollie comes in, wearing pyjamas. He sees his father, watches him, afraid.

Katz wakes. .

Katz Don't be scared . . .

Katz gestures for Ollie to sit with him. The boy remains standing.

You've *grown*. You're a *man*.

Ollie looks at Katz.

Ollie Have you come back?

Fred comes in, wearing his dressing gown. He is holding a baseball bat. Katz stands.

Katz I'm Howard. I let myself in. I fell asleep. I'm sorry. You must be . . .

Fred Fred.

Katz I just wanna talk to Jess . . . OK?

Fred She's asleep.

Katz Can I wait?

They look at each other.

Fred I'll get her . . . Ollie?

Katz He's OK here . . . really. (*Katz gestures to the bat.*) That's mine!

Fred You alright, Ollie?

Ollie nods.

I'll be right back. (*Fred exits.*)

Katz He seems nice. Is he nice . . . ?

Ollie Yeh.

Katz gestures to a small golf bag by the sofa.

Katz Is this yours?

Ollie Yes.

Katz You a golfer?

Ollie Norman takes me.

Katz smiles, pulls out a club. Offers it to Ollie. The boy hesitates.

Katz Show me . . . ?

Katz holds out the club, bows his head.

Please . . . ?

The boy slowly goes to Katz and takes the club.

Jess and Fred come in. Jess in her dressing gown.

Ollie tells me he's a golfer . . .

Jess Yes . . . he's very good. D'you want some coffee?

Katz Perfect, thank you.

Jess (*to Fred*) Would you?

Fred Sure. Ol, breakfast time . . .

Ollie Boiled or scrambled?

Fred Wait and see.

Ollie and Fred exit. Katz watches them go.

Jess What are you doing here?

Katz I was wondering . . . what I most *want* is to come *home* . . . but I know I can't do that . . . I *see* that . . . so . . . could I just come back to *stay* . . . for a while . . . ? Could I live . . . in the spare room – I'd pay rent – and I could take Ollie to school . . . do a bit of cleaning round the house . . . could I just stay . . . and you look after me? Please?

Beat.

Jess What's happened to you?

Katz Is that a 'no'?

Jess It's not possible . . .

Katz nods, understanding.

Katz How's Bern? You seen him?

Jess . . . Yes . . . Nat's pregnant . . .

Katz D'you remember the day Ollie was born? 'Course you do.

Katz picks up his plastic bag, ready to leave.

Jess Do you need some money?

Katz I could do with some cash. Thank you.

Jess I've been trying to contact you. For months.

Katz Yeah, I've been unavailable.

Jess Me and Fred want to get married.

Katz Right. *Mazel tov*. When?

Jess Once you and I . . .

Katz 'Course. Yeh. I'll . . . of course.

Well, that's good. That's how it should be.

I read your Jane Austen.

Jess holds out her hand. Katz reaches for it, misunderstanding the gesture.

Jess Can I have the keys?

Katz gives her his house keys.

Katz I'm really *sorry*. I want you to know that.

Pause.

Jess I'll help you, if you want help.

Katz Nahh, I don't want help. (*slight smile*) I know
what I want.

Casino. Katz stands at a blackjack table.

An Inspector ('Norman') stands nearby.

A dealer ('Natalie') is shuffling.

Low-level lounge muzak in the background.

Inspector This'll be the last shoe of the night, Sir.

Katz What's the time?

Inspector Quarter to four, Sir.

Katz Is it really? Well, I'm gonna *double* my
winnings.

Inspector You're ahead, Sir? Congratulations.

Katz Isn't it *marvellous*? I can't lose!

I *heard* – and I dunno if it's *true* but it *sounds true* –
that up at the Golden Horseshoe last night, this guy
did like a *fortune*, everything he had, like *twenny-five
grand* on roulette . . . and they'd been watching him
on the cameras . . . (*Katz looks up, waves.*) *Hallo.*
And they're pretty damn sure he's gonna *kill* himself,
which they don't really like in casinos 'cos it kinda
gives the impression that PEOPLE ARE DYING IN HERE.

Inspector Sir . . .

Katz So, sure enough, the guy does his dough and
he's practically puking up at the table, he's white and

green – looks like a human *Prozac* – and he slopes off to the Gents with a weird look of *certainty* – the glint of *relief*, the big 'Yes' to 'No'. With me? For some reason, they reckon he's got razor blades – he's come to the *spieler* blades a go-go – *do or die*. And they're *right*. So he's in the Gents, where he instals himself in a cubicle and gets to *work*. Next thing he knows, DOUFF! Security come bursting in, bust down the door and drag the guy out through some private exit and kick him onto the *street*. He's got a blade stuck in each wrist and he's bleeding all over Bayswater. BUT . . . *he did not die in the club*.

So my question is, what's the policy *here*?

Inspector No policy, Sir.

Inspector signals to a Pit Boss ('Bern') to keep an eye on Katz.

Dealer Would you like to cut the cards, Sir?

Katz I'd *love* to cut the cards.

Dealer places cards in the shoe. A Waiter ('Robin') enters.

Waiter Would you like a drink, Sir?

Katz (*to Waiter*) Arsenic.

Waiter Sir?

Katz (*to Waiter*) Straight up. With a twist. Got any matches?

Waiter hands him matches.

Ta. (*to Inspector*) Tell me, Sir, how many boxes is the player *advised* to play?

Inspector One or two, Sir.

Katz I'll play *six*. Hundred on each.

Katz puts £100 on six different boxes.

Inspector nods for the Waiter to go.

Katz puts his yarmulke on, looks up . . .

I wear it for *you*. Not the *little* camera but for *You*:
The Big All Seeing Camera. Uh? For *You*.

A couple come to the table (played by 'Jo' and 'Ellie').

Man Do you mind if we play here?

Katz Step right up.

The woman sits down at the last box.

Man I don't play, my wife plays.

Woman Evening. (*She puts a £5 chip on the box.*)

Katz OK. Big *Fiver*. Enjoy.

The Dealer deals. The Waiter approaches.

Waiter Would you like a drink, Sir?

Man Ooh . . . two hot chocolates, please.

Woman Do you have any?

Waiter I'll see. Two hot chocolates.

Waiter exits. The Dealer turns to the first of Katz's six boxes.

Dealer Thirteen.

Katz Card.

Dealer Seventeen.

Katz Stand. (*next box*) No card. (*next box*) Card. What's that?

Dealer Soft seventeen, Sir.

Katz Card.

   Dealer deals one card.

Dealer Twenty.

Katz Praise the Lord! (*next box*) Card. Yes! (*Next box*) I'll double.

Dealer Doubling, one card only. (*Dealer deals.*) Eighteen.

Katz I thank you. (*next box*) Card.

Dealer Sixteen.

Katz Hmm. (*to Dealer*) What would *you* do?

Dealer It's up to you, Sir.

Katz I so *know* it's up to me. The question I'm asking is what would *you* do?

Dealer I don't play, Sir.

Katz Card.

Dealer Nineteen.

Katz Thank you, love.

   The Dealer turns to the woman, points to her box.

Dealer Eight.

Woman Card please, darling.

Dealer Fifteen.

Woman Hmm . . .

Katz (*friendly*) Excuse me, Madam. May I ask you *not* to take another card? I think it's a small one, let the dealer have it.

Woman Fifteen against a nine, I should take.

Katz I've got six hundred quid on this, you're playing – all due respect – with jelly beans. Please don't take a card. I'll *pay* you not to take a card.

Woman I always take fifteen against a nine. The odds tell you to.

Katz What *are* you, a *pro*?

Inspector Sir.

Katz You've got a *fiver* on the box, I'll give you twenty-five quid *not* to take a card.

Woman It's a principle. *Card*.

Dealer deals her a five.

Dealer Twenty.

Woman (*to Katz*) See!

Dealer No more cards. (*Dealer deals her own card, two . . . and another, ten.*)

Dealer Eleven . . . Twenty-one.

Katz (*to woman*) SEE. SEE! SEE!

Dealer removes the woman's chip and all of Katz's chips.

Woman (*shrugs*) I did the right thing, I played the odds.

Katz You played like a goose.

Inspector Sir.

Katz (*to Dealer*) Chips.

He takes out a big wad of cash, hands it over to the Dealer, who starts to count it.

(*to woman*) If you were '*playing the odds*' you wouldn't *be* here, none of us would *be here*. WE CAN'T WIN!

Katz becomes aware of the 'muzak'.

(*to Pit Boss*) Could you turn down this terrible, terrible noise? It's killing me.

Pit Boss I'm sorry, Sir. It's at a set level.

Katz Can't you just twiddle a knob back there?

(*to Casino in general*) DOES ANYONE LIKE THIS SHIT? ANYONE, ANYWHERE, IN THE WHOLE UNIVERSE?

Pit Boss Sir, I must ask you to calm down.

Katz looks at him, momentarily confused.

Katz Oh, believe me . . . *bro*, this is me BEING CALM.

Pit Boss Please, Sir.

Katz Yeah, yeah.

Dealer turns to Inspector to acknowledge the amount of Katz's cash.

Dealer Two thousand and five.

Inspector nods.

Katz Actually, gimme that five back, might need my cab fare.

Dealer gives Katz £5. She posts the remaining £2000 in a slot on the table and starts to count out chips for Katz.

Dealer Hundreds, Sir?

Katz Yes indeed.

Man Is it *Howard*? Are you Howard Katz?

Katz Used to be . . .?

Man (*offers his hand*) I *thought* it was *you*! Lou, Lou Grossman. We're friends of Jo and Ellie. We met you at the funeral.

Katz *Jungle Lou*?

Lou I went to the jungle, yes! Linda, say hello to Howard!

Linda (*coolly*) Hello.

Katz *Kalooki Linda*? (I'm in hell.) Hey, how's the *archery*, Lou?

Lou Nyah, I had to stop. I was pulling all my muscles. (*Lou vaguely illustrates.*)

Katz Shame.

Lou (*referring to yarmulke*) I didn't know you were *frum*.

Katz Oh yeah, well, I've *become frum* – frum as fuck, quite frankly.

Inspector Sir.

Katz He can *take it*, this man's fought *lions* in the jungle.

Lou (*concerned*) Howard, how's your mother?

Katz Dead. Died yesterday.

Lou Really?

Katz No. Not *really*.

Dealer finishes counting Katz's chips and places them in front of him.

Dealer Two thousand.

The Manager arrives at the table (actor playing 'Jess'). She whispers to the Pit Boss then turns to Katz:

Manager Sir . . .

Katz Look who's here! I found a way, darling! Russian roulette!

Manager This'll be the last hand of the night, Sir.

Katz You what? (*Gestures to Inspector.*) Old 'laughing boy' said it was the last *shoe*.

Manager It's five to four, Sir. I'm sorry.

Katz Yeah, yeah. What's the max?

Pit Boss Two thousand on the box, Sir.

Katz Magnificent. I have exactly two thousand.

Katz places £2000 on one box. A big, high stack. The casino floor goes quiet . . .

Dealer Two thousand on the box, Sir?

Katz Yes indeed. (*to God*) Do or die, your choice, *pal*.

The Dealer deals, then points to Katz's box.

Dealer Soft thirteen.

Katz Card.

Dealer deals him one card. Katz sees it and celebrates.

Dealer Twenty. No more cards, Sir?

Katz Twenty. I am content.

Dealer points to Linda's box.

Dealer Twelve.

Linda Hmm . . .

Katz Oh no . . .

Dealer Card twelve, Madam?

Linda Hmm . . .

Katz Oh no no no no . . .

Dealer Card twelve?

Katz Of course she doesn't want a card on *twelve*. *No one* takes twelve against a *three*.

Linda No tens out . . .

Katz (*of Dealer*) So let *her* have them.

Dealer Card, Madam?

Katz Don't encourage her.

Inspector Sir.

Katz Listen, *pal*, I've got *two grand* sitting here. This is my *life*. Linda, lovely Linda, don't take a card . . .

Pit Boss Sir, please let the lady decide what she wants to do.

Katz She's no lady.

Linda Lou?

Lou (*shrugs*) 'You gotta do what you gotta do.'

Linda Card.

Katz NO!

Dealer Twenty-two. (*Dealer removes Linda's cards and chip.*)

Katz *See?*

Dealer No more cards.

Freeze. Katz looks round the stage, disorientated. He sees his family but they are all strangers. He looks up.

Katz (*to God*) Yes or no?

The 'freeze' breaks. Dealer deals to herself . . . a ten, a two and a six.

Dealer Thirteen . . . fifteen . . . twenty-one.

Dealer removes all of Katz's cards and chips.

Pause.

Katz (*to Linda*) She'd've bust. You took the ten, you mad trout. You took her ten, she'd've bust. (*flat*) You've killed me.

The Waiter returns.

Waiter (*to Lou*) I'm sorry, Sir, no hot chocolate.

Lou '*C'est la vie.*' Thanks for trying.

The Waiter goes.

Linda (*to Katz*) You brought the table bad luck.

Lou Lindy, let's go now . . .

Linda There's *evil* in you, it transmits to the cards.

Katz Excuse me?

Linda You heard.

Katz Evil?

Lou Lindy, darling sweetheart –

Linda (*sharp*) *Shush* Lou! (*to Katz*) I've played this game forty years. I know your type. Your mother *knew*, she knew about *you*.

Katz (*to Pit Boss*) Are you going to protect me from this shit?

Pit Boss Sir –

Katz Listen, Mrs *Rasputin* –

Pit Boss Sir –

Katz Will you *stop* calling me 'Sir'? I am not a 'Sir' and I will never *be* a 'Sir'.

The Pit Boss and Inspector begin to usher Katz away.

Pit Boss I must ask you to leave, Sir.

Katz It's all right, I'm going. I am *leaving* the building. *Evil* is leaving the building. (*to Lou and Linda*) YOU KILLED ME.

Katz is ejected onto the street. He starts to walk.

Katz Evil has left the building. Beware Leicester Square, evil is amongst you, the corrupter of youth, the stealer of souls – Raging Yid is on the *street* – CLEAN THESE STREETS!

Katz swigs from his bottle of rum. It starts to rain.

That's it ... RAIN ... PERFECT ... Piss all over me ... Very KIND ...

Rain. Thunder. Lightning. Katz raises his face to the sky.

DROWN ME you *God*!

What kind of God kills an old dad with love in his heart?

What d'you do to my *mum*? YOU BASTARD!

NO ONE BELIEVES IN YOU. NO ONE LOVES YOU.

Is this what you want? Have me screaming here like some RAT?

Some wet rat shitting himself in the dark and the rain?

Just blood and water and bone endlessly wandering ... NO MORE!

GIVE ME THE COURAGE!

Katz glugs from the bottle, pours rum all over himself.

Burn me to nothing and vanish my ashes.

He takes a box of matches and starts to strike them.

Strike my life from the books and *unborn* me.

The matches won't strike.

Fucking bollocks.

STRIKE ME DOWN WITH LIGHTNING!

He raises his arms to conduct lightning onto himself.

No?

NO?

Then what?

WHAT DO YOU WANT FROM ME?

WHAT DO YOU WANT FROM ME?

Katz howls. Glugs. Stumbles. Falls.

I WANT MY DAD.

I WANT MY MUM.

I WANT MY WIFE.

I WANT MY SON.

He passes out by a park bench. Face down.

And now it's night, in the park, in the present.

Katz sits on the park bench. Swigs from his bottle of rum. Puts it on the ground.

He opens his grey plastic bag, takes out a bottle of pills and places it next to the bottle.

Next, he takes out a cut-throat razor. He opens the razor and examines the blade. Places it on the ground.

He takes his yarmulke from his pocket, puts it on.

He sits, contemplating his 'weapons' laid out before him.

Robin enters. He carries a McDonald's bag.

He sees the 'weapons'. Looks at Katz, then sits on the bench.

Robin starts to eat. Katz looks at him.

Robin offers a Chicken McNugget to Katz. Katz declines.

Robin Starving yourself? Original, like it.

You been here all day?

Katz nods. Robin eats. Looks at Katz.

Wanna tell me about it?

Katz Why d'you *care*?

Robin I told you. I know about this. I went there.

What is it, little mid-life crisis?

Katz Yeah. But it's bigger than me. (*Katz looks at his 'weapons'.*) What did *you* do?

Robin shows Katz his wrists.

Robin Lid of a soup can. Go *home*.

Katz Haven't got one.

Beat.

Robin So make a new one.

Katz No strength.

Robin So kill yourself.

Katz Leave me in peace and I *will*.

Robin continues to eat.

Robin You ain't got the *balls*, mate. If you were *serious* you'd be *alone*, in a *room*. You're sitting here like a big fat cry for help.

Katz I will hit you. I swear, I will hit you.

Robin Oh, what a *man*.

Katz grabs him by the throat.

Katz Don't make me hit you.

Beat.

Robin (*calmly*) Grow up.

Katz lets him go. Gestures an apology.

Katz paces briefly, comes to rest.

Katz I'm a fool.

I'm a failure.

I've lost everything.

I've sat here, all day, watched the people come and go . . . and I am so . . . (*Katz puts his hand on his heart.*) How do they do it? How on *earth* do they *do* it?

And . . . everyone . . . *reminds* me of everyone else. D'you know what I mean?

Robin No, mate.

Katz (*sighs*) Every time I aspire to a little poetry, a little grandeur, the world farts in my face.

Robin hands him the pill bottle.

Robin Off you go.

Katz swallows a couple of pills, hands the pill bottle back to Robin.

You might need a few *more* than that.

Katz Eh? I've got a *headache*. Hangover.

Katz swigs some rum.

Robin Wanna fag?

Katz nods. Takes a cigarette from Robin.

You got a place to sleep?

Katz No. I'll be alright . . .

Katz offers his bottle to Robin. Robin swigs, hands it back.

How . . . how did you get to be so *calm*?

Robin Practice.

Katz looks at Robin, curious.

Katz What keeps you going?

Robin Fame. I'm gonna be famous. Dunno how, but I'm gonna be . . .

Katz thinks, decides against.

Katz Good luck to you.

Robin I gotta go . . .

Katz Thank you.

Robin (*shrugs*) You'd do the same for me.

Katz Maybe I would. What's your name?

Robin Robin.

They listen to the distant traffic.

Katz I've got this . . . *boy*. He's ten. And I remember the day he was born but . . . I can't remember the *feeling* . . .

Have you got my watch?

Robin Sold it.

Beat.

Katz Robin . . . would you give me a hug?

Robin (*smiles*) Fuck off.

Robin exits. Katz looks up to God for a short while.

Katz Maybe I'll be a rabbi. (*Sneers.*) Would you like that?

He untucks his shirt and scratches his belly button.

You want us to *live* . . . don't you?

He examines some fluff on his finger, flicks it away.

You didn't take the *ten*, Linda *Grossman* took the *ten*, that's what *happened*.

Isn't it?

He starts to pack up his 'weapons'.

Will you answer?

Just once?

Please?

He looks at the razor then packs it away.

Arsehole.

He removes his yarmulke, starts to wander off with his plastic bag.

He stops.

Silence.

Then, slowly, he begins to remember . . .

(*Softly*) . . . I remember . . . I *remember* now . . . thank you, *God* . . . don't answer . . . don't do a *thing* . . . for you have *done* your mighty work this day . . . *relax* . . . put your slippers on, mate.

Dad . . . you're a bloody *grandad*, you old *beauty* . . . a *boy* . . . eighteen bloody hours . . . seven pounds, four ounces . . . will you tell Bern?

Uncle Bern, can you believe it?

And Norm . . . tell Norm he's the *godfather*.

Hey, put Mum on . . . Hallo, Granny . . . Good morning, *Granny* . . . thank *you* . . . for having *me* . . . my God . . . *thank you* . . . Jess is *fine* . . . she was marvellous, heroic as ever . . . the *pain* of it . . . I nearly *fainted* . . . Yes, I'm all right . . . it's a *miracle* . . . he's *beautiful* . . . a strange little soldier come home from the war . . .

I understand *everything* . . . everything has shape and pattern and *substance* . . . everything is meant to *be* . . . we're . . . *we're not alone* . . . we're *connected* to every living *thing* . . . there's some *moss* here, in a crack in the pavement – and I *love* this *moss* . . . I'm kissing the moss, Mum – no, I'm not *licking* it . . .

Can you *believe* it? I can't believe *any* of it. And it's true.

Silence.

Katz takes a drag on his cigarette. The memory gone.

He thinks for a while.

To live.

I want to live.

Tell me how to live.

Blackout.